TasteandSee

100% Paleo, Primal, Zone,

Gluten-free, & Dairy-free Recipes

Thank you Michael for believing in this book and dreaming with me!

Thank you Jason & Tori Benham, David & Lori Benham,
Steve & Jess Pinkerton, & Brad Nelson for the encouragement to take on this project and the much needed taste-testing along the way!

Thank you, Dr. Michael Brown for all your help! You were a blessing beyond words!

Thank you, Steve Alt! You are an amazing editor and made the correction process a laughing experience!

Thank you Sheree Moitoso (Mother) for your encouragement and prayers! You are an incredible mother and friend!

Thank you, Gregg Montella for your creative input throughout this entire project. It meant a lot to have you involved.

**To the greatest kids ever: Aliya, Aiden, & Maya,
May you cultivate a lifestyle of eating healthy foods
while making sure they taste good, too! I love you guys!**

This book should not be considered a substitute for advice from a medical professional or nutritionists. Please consult a doctor or wellness center before making any extreme changes to your diet.

Taste & See
Copyright © 2012 Lisa Lubanovic
Photographs copyright © 2012 Lisa Lubanovic

All Rights Reserved.
No portion of this book may be copied in any form without written permission from the author.

Library of Congress Cataloging-in-Publication
ISBN: 978-0-9851201-0-8

Visit us at:
www.TasteandSeeFoods.com

TABLE OF CONTENTS

TESTIMONIALS   7

INTRODUCTION   8

BREAKFAST   12

SOUPS & SALADS   29

ENTREES   45

SIDE DISHES   73

DESSERTS   89

TESTIMONIALS

"When I started having babies, I began putting on extra weight pretty quickly. By the time I had 4 babies in 8 years I had gained nearly 70lbs. I tried several different diets throughout the last couple of years but always gave up because I never saw the weight come off. I began hearing through friends who were having some similar health problems that taking gluten out of their diet almost eliminated their issue. I decided it was worth a try and almost immediately took gluten, sugar and dairy out of my diet. Not only did I lose 44 lbs in 5 months, but I have seen a few health issues resolved. 8 months later I am still following this diet along with exercise and I couldn't be happier with my choice. It feels so wonderful to be healthy!"
Jamie Jessee, Teacher and mother of four

"As a mom, pharmacist, and food connoisseur, its so exciting to know someone is out there working on recipes that are both healthy and taste delicious. Lisa has tried many different combinations in the search for tasty new recipes supporting the paleo diet and diets with food restrictions. As a pharmacist reviewing these recipes, it was obvious she did her research and we can all benefit from the knowledge she has gained in creating new foods! How exciting it is that she is putting this information out there for the rest of us to benefit from!" Now we just have to make the recipes she created and enjoy!
Kristen DeSantis, Pharmacist and mother of four

"Serving in Afghanistan 5 years ago, I was nearly thrown out of my jeep. A seatbelt saved my life. Very quickly I realized that to continue my work and increase my chances of surviving, I needed to lose 40 pounds of fat and be able to RUN. Since turning 25, weight came on and stayed on. Working out didn't fix it; fad dieting did little in the long run either. Then I joined Crossfit and learned the Zone diet. I was working out less (but more intensively), eating better (and more often), and within a week was feeling and seeing the results. Crossfit, combined with the Zone principles of 1) Portion Control, 2) Balanced intake of carbs, proteins, and fats, and 3) Not spiking my blood-sugar through smart eating, led me to lose 30 pounds of fat and finally gain the 15 pounds of muscle I'd been looking for. Two years later, in Pakistan, I was put to the test, and being able to run literally saved my life. At 34, I'm fit, enjoying life, food, and work. I wholeheartedly recommend this cookbook, in combination with learning the basic principles of Zone. It could save your life -- it did mine!"
Gregg Montella, Director of One Heart International Mission

"With Lisa's help and encouragement, I have lost weight and eaten healthy food at the same time. In fact, I have been amazed by the results and honestly can't believe how quickly I started to notice a difference in my appearance and the way I felt. And, I did it without starving myself or having to deal with the cravings for food one typically gets when attempting to diet. I highly recommend Lisa's book and her valuable insights."
S.J. Hill, Author and international speaker
www.s.j.hill.com

"Shortly after I had my second baby, I felt different. At first I thought it was hormones and exhaustion so I gave it a few weeks. About 4 weeks postpartum I got an infection and was prescribed a antibiotic. For the next year I was prescribed 9 rounds of antibiotics for numerous infections. No one ever thought to ask why I was having infections, antibiotics were always the answer. I believe this is what destroyed my gut! Along with infections and low immunity, I was constantly blacking out upon standing, extremely fatigued, dizzy, having extreme pain in my stomach and catching every sickness floating around. At the start of the year my kids got strep throat. I got it soon after, and over the next week my tired immune system couldn't fight it off and it turned into scarlet fever. I went to the doctor and they said it had gone into my kidneys... and of course prescribed more antibiotics. I finally decided to see a nutritionist and holistic doctor. The first thing he told me to do was to eliminate all flour, grains, and sugar. He did some tests and found that I was malnourished. My stomach lining was so inflamed that it wasn't absorbing nutrients. My skin was starting to look yellow! With in days of following this diet, I hadn't had one black out or felt dizzy. After about six weeks, my doctor did another test to see if my stomach was absorbing nutrients and it was! He then started me on a regiment of supplements and probiotics to replenish what the antibiotics have destroyed over the past year. It took two years of recovery, they had found that my adrenal glands were significantly weakened, and I had in fact, a wheat allergy. I had developed candida overgrowth, strep B overgrowth, and a compromised immune system. Wheat flour and sugar were feeding the problem. Because I was eating gluten free and organic foods and NO sugar, my body began to heal and we were able to destroy the bacterial overgrowths using some natural treatments. I'm not going to lie, it wasn't easy at first, and kind of depressing when you realize how much of your favorite foods are eliminated from your diet. But, I was determined to get better! A lot of research and scouring the internet for recipes, cooking gluten and sugar free became second nature. I actually enjoy food now! Especially when I know it is helping my body heal. I was also very surprised to see how well my family adapted to my new diet. My kids love when I cook and my husband has even mentioned how he enjoys some of my gf versions over the wheat ones! I'm so thankful for my friend Lisa's new book, it is an amazing compilation of tried and true recipes that are not only delicious, but easy to make and healthy! No more scouring the internet, this book is all you need!"
Lindsey Collins, Business owner and mother of three

INTRODUCTION

MY STORY

Healthy food can and *should* taste good. However, for years I settled for what I thought to be the inevitable: eating healthy means giving up great-tasting foods. I was willing to sacrifice flavor for better health--and, I did so for many years. But, I have discovered I don't have to eat poor tasting foods, so now I thankfully and happily don't!

My journey began around the age of six. As my complaints of stomach pain grew, so did the visits to the doctor and the seemingly endless testing. At age sixteen, I had my first colonoscopy and barium testing, among many other procedures too embarrassing to list. Each specialist left us without answers as to the cause of my increasingly serious illness. I was in chronic pain with scary symptoms and found little to no relief in any of the medications that were prescribed. Once in college, I adopted a mirage of odd diets in hopes of self-healing. This left me unable to maintain a healthy weight, with periods of severe dizziness and fainting....and, still no relief. After I was married, I continued to battle while seeking more medical treatment. Every doctor agreed with the previous one that there was something very much wrong, but none could identify the source of the illness.

Many nights, after I would finally fall asleep, I would be awakened to the sound of my husband praying for God to heal me. He was a source of strength and compassion during these challenging times. It was after one of these nights that my husband suggested that I get tested for a gluten allergy. My test came back screaming: positive! I planned to test a gluten-free diet for a couple of weeks and survey my results. Honestly, a small part of me hoped that I would show little to no results; allowing my bread binging days to live on. But, as I cleansed my system of gluten I was relieved of each and every symptom. I remember describing to my husband how odd, and even light, my stomach felt. I realized this was a feeling of healing...of an absence of pain; one that I had learned to live with for the past twenty-four years.

A pain and symptom-free life was a strong motivator to keep the wheat at bay. But like all good motivators, the temptation must never be allowed to out grow them. The short list of foods I could eat soon left me bored and unsatisfied. I was making separate meals for my family and feeling sorry for myself while looking at the pitiful pile of food sitting on my plate. They sported plates full of foods, flavors, and aromas I loved. Mine wasn't even worth mentioning.

However, this all changed the day I decided to get creative and make recipes that tasted better than the ones I so loved. This turned into a several month long project. I would get so excited for my husband to come home from work and try my latest concoction. If he liked it, I sent leftovers with him to work for others to enjoy and critique. After a couple of months of this, a few friends suggested I put my recipes in book form and share them with others. The following pages are the fruit of my journey to a healthier me.

I believe that health goes so much deeper than just ones' body and includes the mind and soul. Each page has a small section at the bottom meant to inspire and encourage; ultimately bringing about a healthier you! I pray that this book helps you to find better health and enjoyment in the wonderful foods we have so been graced with in our everyday lives.

Blessings galore!
Lisa Lubanovic

Lisa Lubanovic is the happily married wife of Michael Lubanovic, and mother and home school teacher of three incredible children. Her journey to find better health for herself and others stirred her to write a cookbook that marries both exceptional flavors and natural ingredients. While she has a passion to cook, she can also be found knee-deep in her latest art project, enjoying the outdoors with her family, discovering ways to involve her children in impacting the lives of others in her city, as well as, overseas, and growing closer to the One who forever won her heart, her Lord and Savior, Jesus Christ.

BREAKFAST

BACON PEPPERED OMELET
Start your morning with this quick and simple protein-packed meal!

Ingredients:

4 eggs
3-4 pieces of cooked nitrate-free bacon, cut into small pieces
1/3 cup roasted red pepper
1 tbs olive oil
1 tsp black pepper
1/4 tsp onion powder
Salt, to taste

Directions:

1. Oil a medium-sized frying pan.
2. Once oil is heated, add eggs and heat until eggs begin to set.
3. Add remaining ingredients and cook until egg is almost done.
4. Fold egg in half to create folded-omelet shape and cook until egg is fully cooked.
5. Salt and pepper to taste.

Serves 2

"Speak tenderly to them. Let there be kindness in your face, in your eyes, in your smile, in the warmth of your greeting. Always have a cheerful smile. Don't only give your care, but give your heart as well." Mother Teresa

BUTTERNUTTY PANCAKES
A delicious way to eat your veggies first thing in the morning!

Ingredients:

1 1/2 cups butternut squash, cooked and mashed
3 cups almond flour
2 eggs
1 tsp baking powder
1 tsp baking soda
2 1/2 tsp cinnamon
1 3/4 cups almond milk, unsweetened vanilla
2 tbs Nutiva ® Coconut Manna
Coconut oil, for pan

Directions:

1. In a large bowl, combine ingredients in order listed. Batter will be thick.
2. Spoon batter onto oiled, heated skillet. Spread batter flat with spoon. Batter is very sticky and may pull away from skillet if you are not careful. The key is to slowly flatten batter filling in any holes.
3. Cook for 3 min. on each side. This batter does not bubble like traditional pancake batter.
4. Serve with fresh fruit or pure maple syrup.

Serves 6

"This is how God showed his love among us: He sent his one and only Son into the world that we might live through him." 1 John 4:9

B'EGG'CON RINGS
Gourmet breakfast made simple!

Ingredients:

8 slices of nitrate-free turkey bacon
1 roma tomato sliced into 1/2 inch slices
4 eggs
2 tsp chopped onion
1/4 tsp seasoning salt
Pepper to taste

Directions:

1. Preheat oven to 325°F.
2. Heat bacon in a skillet over medium heat for about 4 minutes on each side.
3. With some of the fat from the bacon, grease the insides of 4 ramekins, or small oven-safe bowl.
4. Place a tomato in the bottom of each ramekin, and wrap the inside with 2 bacon strips.
5. Next, crack an egg into the center of each cup and sprinkle tops with chopped onion and seasoning salt.
6. Bake for 20 minutes.
7. Can be served in or out of ramekins.

Serves 4

"The presence of hope in the invincible sovereignty of God drives out fear." John Piper

OMELET MUFFINS

Finally, a way to take your favorite omelet to-go!

Ingredients:

6 eggs
1-2 Italian sausage links (about 1/2 cup)
1/2 cup frozen chopped spinach, thawed and drained
1/8 tsp ground pepper
1/8 cup water
1/2 tsp chopped onions

Directions:

1. Preheat oven to 350 °F.
2. Line 6 muffin tins with paper liners.
3. Remove casing from raw sausage links and discard.
4. In a large bowl, beat eggs.
5. Add sausage, spinach, pepper, water, and onions to eggs.
6. Spoon egg mixture into paper-lined tins.
7. Bake for 18-20 minutes or until a toothpick can be cleanly inserted and removed from center of muffin.

Serves 6

"[God] will use you to accomplish great things on the condition that you believe much more in His love than in your own weakness." Mother Teresa

ALMOND PANCAKES
Everything tastes better with almonds!

Ingredients:

1 1/2 cups almond flour
1/2 cup apple sauce
1 tsp Nutiva ® Coconut Manna
2 eggs
1/4 cup water
1 tsp coconut oil
1 tsp baking soda

Directions:

1. Mix all ingredients together in a large bowl.
2. This batter will be slightly thicker than traditional flour pancakes, but is perfect for making fun-shapes.
3. Using a scooped-measuring cup, pour 1/3 cup batter into skillet .
4. Flip pancake when center begins to bubble.
5. Garnish with fresh berries!

Serves 4

"God cannot give us a happiness and peace apart from Himself, because it is not there. There is no such thing." C.S. Lewis

ZUCCHINI CARROT MUFFINS

Double or triple this recipes and freeze the leftovers. Great for breakfast or a snack

Ingredients:

2 cups almond flour
2 tsp baking soda
1 tbs cinnamon
1 cup prunes
1 cup shredded zucchini
3 eggs
1 tsp apple cider vinegar
1/4 cup coconut oil
1 1/2 cups carrots, shredded
3/4 cup walnuts, finely chopped
1/3 cup xylitol
1/2 cup almond milk, unsweetened vanilla

Directions:

1. Preheat oven to 350 °F.
2. In a small bowl, combine almond flour, baking soda, and cinnamon.
3. In a food processor, combine prunes, eggs, vinegar, oil, xylitol, and almond milk.
4. Mix wet and dry ingredients together in a large bowl. Add zucchini, carrots, and walnuts and mix until well combined.
5. Spoon mixture into paper-lined muffin tins.
6. Bake for 25 minutes.

Makes 36 muffins

"To love God does not mean to meet His needs, but rather to delight in Him and to be captivated by His glorious power and grace, and to value Him above all other things on earth." John Piper

APPLE NUT MUFFINS
Pure protein goodness!

Ingredients:

1 cup almond butter
1 cup sliced raw almonds
1 cup pure coconut milk
1 whole apple, chopped
2 cups unsweetened shredded coconut
3 eggs
2 tbs pure maple syrup
2 tsp ground cinnamon

Directions:

1. Preheat oven to 350 °F.
2. In a large bowl, combine almond butter, milk, eggs, and maple syrup.
3. Stir in almonds, apple , coconut and cinnamon.
4. Pour batter into paper-lined muffin tins.
5. Bake for 15 minutes or until muffins are firm on top.

Makes 24 muffins

"For the Lord God is our sovereign protector. The Lord bestows favor and honor; he withholds no good thing from those who have integrity." Psalm 84:11

BERRY BUTTER SMOOTHIE
Dessert for breakfast? We won't tell your taste buds this isn't a milkshake!

Ingredients:

1 cup frozen sweet dark cherries
1 cup frozen mango
3 cups almond milk, unsweetened vanilla
2 tbs almond butter
1 tsp pure vanilla
1 tbs Nutiva ® Coconut Manna

Directions:

1. Put all ingredients, except Coconut Manna, in a blender.
2. Blend until smooth and creamy.
3. Add Coconut Manna and blend until well combined.

Serves 6

The secret of the mystery is: God is always greater. No matter how great we think Him to be, His love is always greater. -Brennan Manning

NUTTY COCONUT GRANOLA
Cereal never tasted this good! Eat with your favorite nut milk and fresh fruit.

Ingredients:

2 tbs melted coconut oil
2 1/2 tbs pure vanilla extract
1/2 tsp pure almond extract
2 tsp local honey
1 cup unsweetened coconut flakes
1/4 cup raw sliced almonds
1/4 cup raw pecan pieces
1/2 tsp cinnamon
1 pinch nutmeg

Directions:

1. Preheat oven to 350 °F.
2. In a large bowl, mix liquid ingredients together.
3. Mix in dry ingredients in order listed.
4. Bake for 7-10 minutes, Stir and continue baking for an additional 7-10 or until golden brown. Watch closely to make sure granola does not burn.
5. Allow to cool for 1-2 hours on counter top before storing in an airtight container.

"But whatever you do, find the God-centered, Christ-exalting, Bible-saturated passion of your life, and find your way to say it and live for it and die for it. And you will make a difference that lasts. You will not waste your life." John Piper

PUMPKIN PROTEIN MUFFINS

These are even tastier when warmed!

Ingredients:

1 1/2 cups almond flour
1 tsp baking powder
1 tsp baking soda
2 1/2 tbs cinnamon
2 scoops of vanilla (non-dairy) hemp protein powder
1 cup of canned pumpkin
1/2 cup honey
3 eggs

Directions:

1. Preheat over to 350 °F.
2. In a small bowl, combine dry ingredients; while combining wet ingredients together in a large bowl.
3. Add dry ingredients to large bowl and mix well.
4. Pour batter into lined cupcake pans and bake for approximately 20 minutes.

Makes 24 muffins

"Praise the Lord, O my soul, and forget not all his benefits— who forgives all your sins and heals all your diseases, who redeems your life from the pit and crowns you with love and compassion, who satisfies your desires with good things so that your youth is renewed like the eagle's." Psalm 103:2-5

FRUITY COCONUT SMOOTHIE
Simple and refreshing!

Ingredients:

1 1/2 cups almond milk, unsweetened vanilla
11/2 cups fresh or frozen strawberries
1/2 cup fresh or frozen blueberries

Directions:

1. Blend all ingredients until smooth.
2. Garnish with blueberries.
3. Leftovers can be frozen into fruit popsicles.

Serves 3-4

"For I am convinced that neither death nor life, neither angels nor demons, neither the present nor the future, nor any powers, neither height nor depth, nor anything else in all creation, will be able to separate us from the love of God that is in Christ Jesus our Lord." Romans 8:38-39

PEACH COBBLER SMOOTHIE

Savor the taste of summer year around.

Ingredients:

16 oz frozen bag of peaches
1 tbs honey
1/4 tsp vanilla
1/8 tsp cinnamon
Pinch of nutmeg
1/2 cup almond milk, unsweetened vanilla
2 tbs maple syrup

Directions:

1. Blend all ingredients until smooth.
2. Serve immediately

Serves 3-4

"May the God of your hope so fill you with all joy and peace in believing that by the power of the Holy Spirit you may abound and be overflowing with hope." Romans 15: 13

BETTER THAN OATMEAL

This hearty dish will have you wondering why you ever loved traditional cereal!

Ingredients:

1/2 cup pecans
1/2 cup walnuts
2 tbs flax seed
2 tsp ground cinnamon
1 tsp ground cloves
1 pinch ginger
1 tbs almond butter
1 banana, mashed; optional
3 eggs
1/4 cup almond milk, unsweetened vanilla
Maple syrup, sweeten to taste

Directions:

1. In a food processor, grind nuts until they reach a coarse consistency.
2. Add spices and set aside.
3. In a medium-sized bowl whisk together eggs and milk. Add banana and almond butter, mix well.
4. Pour nut and egg mixtures into a large saucepan and heat over medium-low heat.
5. Stir constantly for 2-3 minutes until mixture thickens.
6. Remove from heat and sweeten with maple syrup.
7. If desired, add fresh fruit and almond milk.

Serves 2

"Jesus did not come to make God's love possible, but to make God's love visible." Anonymous

CINNAMON RAISIN BREAD
Use raisins or your favorite dried fruit.

Ingredients:

3/4 cup almond flour
1 1/2 cups arrowroot flour
1 cup raisins
1 1/2 tsp cinnamon
1 egg
1/8 cup honey
3/4 cup unsweetened, vanilla almond milk
1/4 tsp baking soda
1/4 tsp baking powder
Coconut oil, for pan

Directions:

1. Preheat oven to 350°F.
2. Mix all wet ingredients in a small bowl and set aside.
3. Combine all dry ingredients together in a large bowl.
4. Stir in wet ingredients and roll into a ball.
5. Place in an oiled bread pan and bake for 30 minutes.

Serves 6

"Our desires, affections, pursuits, all that we say and do, all that we love or hate, are to be measured by this single criterion and subordinated to this one end: happiness in God."
Sam Storms

BANANA BREAD

A difficult bread to live without! This recipe reinvents an all-time favorite!

Ingredients:

1 cup almond flour
1 cup arrowroot flour
2 ripe bananas
1 1/2 tsp cinnamon
1/4 tsp nutmeg
1 egg
1/8 cup honey
1/8 cup maple syrup
1/4 tsp baking soda
1/4 tsp baking powder

Directions:

1. Preheat oven to 350°F.
2. Mix all wet ingredients in a small bowl and set aside.
3. In a large bowl combine all dry ingredients.
4. Stir in wet ingredients and roll into a ball.
5. Place in an oiled bread pan and bake for 30 minutes.

Serves 4-6

"O, give thanks unto the Lord, for He is good." I Chronicles 16:34

SOUPS & SALADS

BLACKBERRY VINAIGRETTE
Add to any bed of greens for a delicious salad.

Ingredients:

1/4 cup red wine
1 medium shallot
1 tbs honey, to taste
1 tbs dijon mustard
1 tbs dried parsley
1/4 tsp salt
1/4 tsp ground pepper
1/2 cup extra-virgin, cold pressed olive oil
1 cup blackberries

Directions:

1. In a medium bowl combine vinegar, shallot, honey, mustard, parsley, salt, and pepper.
2. Whisk all ingredients together, slowly adding oil.
3. Once dressing is well combined, stir in blueberries.
4. Add all ingredients at once to a food processor and pulse until fully combined. You can replace a food processor with a blender for this step.
5. Serve over greens and add nuts for protein. Garnish with blueberries.

"God created us so that the joy He has in Himself might be ours." Sam Storms

SALMON CURRY SALAD

Not only is this salad packed with protein and flavor, it is also easy to prepare!

Ingredients for salad:

1 six oz salmon fillet, fresh or canned
1 tbs coconut oil
2 cups baby spinach
1 avocado, cut into medium chunks
2 tbs sliced almonds
1 tbs chopped green onions
2 roma tomatoes
1 lemon, juiced
1/4 tsp garlic powder

Ingredients for dressing:

2-3 tbs coconut milk
1/2 tsp parsley
3/4 tsp curry seasoning
1/4 tsp cinnamon
Pinch of cayenne pepper, to taste
4 tbs red wine vinegar
2 tsp honey

Directions for salad:

1. Pan-fry salmon in oil and seasoning with spices; cooking fully.
2. Using a fork, flake meat.
3. Add tomatoes, lemon juice, and garlic powder. Cook until tomatoes are tender.
4. Pour over a bed of spinach and top with almonds, avocado, and green onions.
5. Add dressing and serve.

Directions for dressing:

1. In a small bowl, whisk all ingredients together until fully combined.
2. Pour over salad.
3. Refrigerate any unused dressing.

Serves 1 as a meal, 2 as a side

"Rejoice in the Lord always [delight, gladden yourselves in Him]; again I say, Rejoice!"
Philippians 4:4

SHRIMP & AVOCADO SALAD

Seafood and guacamole lovers beware! Eat this as a side... or, meal if you can't resist!

Ingredients:

1 lb. cooked shrimp, peeled and deveined
4 ripe avocados
4 ripe roma tomatoes
2 green onions, chopped
1 large yellow pepper, chopped
1 Hungarian hot or Jalapeno pepper, seeded and chopped
3 cloves of garlic, crushed
2 limes, juiced
1/2 cup olive oil
1/4 cup fresh cilantro, chopped
Salt and pepper, to taste

Directions:

1. Prepare vegetables and place in a medium-sized bowl with shrimp.
2. Add lime juice, oil, cilantro, salt ,and pepper. Stir carefully, making sure to not mash avocados.
3. Chill for at least 2 hours before serving to allow the flavors to blend.

Serves 4

"Our circumstances are not an accurate reflection of God's goodness. Whether life is good or bad, God's goodness, rooted in His character, is the same." Helen Grace Lescheid

PROTEIN & GREEN SALAD

Build your muscles while treating your taste buds. This salad is oh, so good!

Ingredients for salad:

5 slices bacon, cut into 1/2 inch pieces
4 boneless, skinless chicken breasts, cubed
Seasoning salt, to taste
1 head romaine lettuce, chopped
1 avocado, cut into small chunks,
1/4 cup red onion
1/4 cup walnuts, chopped
1 apple, cut into small chunks
1/4 cup almond slices

Ingredients for dressing:

1/4 cup white balsamic vinegar
2 tbs red wine vinegar
1 shallot, minced
1 garlic clove, minced
1 tsp mustard
Salt and pepper, to taste
1/3 cup extra virgin olive oil

Directions for salad:

1. Heat bacon in a pan until crisp. Place bacon on paper towel to absorb grease.
2. In the same pan (do not remove bacon grease), add chicken and season liberally with seasoning salt. Cook until meat is browned.
3. Add chicken and bacon to a salad bowl with romaine lettuce, avocado, onion, walnuts, almonds, and apple.
4. Add dressing and toss.

Directions, for dressing:

1. Mix all ingredients together in a food processor, or whisk by hand.
2. Pour dressing over salad.
3. Refrigerate after using.

"God's greatest interest is to glorify the wealth of His grace by making sinners happy in Him."
John Piper

MEXICAN SOUP

Salsa, baby! This is a fiesta waiting to happen in your mouth!

Ingredients:

1 avocado
2 -3 roma tomatoes
1 cup water
1 cup red, green, or orange pepper (fresh or frozen)
1 cup baby bella mushrooms
1 tsp dried onion
1 garlic clove, minced
1 lime, juiced
1/4 cup fresh cilantro
2 seasoned cooked chicken breasts, cubed, optional

Directions:

1. In a food processor, blend everything together except chicken (if you are adding chicken).
2. Pour into a soup pot and heat over medium heat, stirring often.

Serves 2

"The enjoyment of God is the only happiness with which our souls can be satisfied."
Jonathan Edwards

VEGGIE CHICKEN SOUP

This hearty soup is the perfect dish for a cold or rainy day!

Ingredients:

2 cups all-natural chicken broth
4 boneless, skinless grilled chicken breasts, cubed
1 cup water
3 medium carrots
1 small sweet potato, peeled and cubed
1 cup cauliflower, chopped
1/2 of 1 small parsnip, peeled and sliced
14 oz. can lite coconut milk
1/4 tsp cinnamon
1/2 tsp oregano
Pepper, to taste

Directions:

1. Bring chicken broth and water to a boil in a medium soup pot.
2. Add carrots, sweet potatoes, cauliflower, and parsnips and cook until softened.
3. Pour coconut milk into soup and cook for another 3-5 minutes.
4. Pour soup into a blender or a food processor and blend until pureed.
5. Return soup to pot and add grilled chicken. Simmer for 20 min. and serve.

Serves 6

"Man's chief end is to glorify God by enjoying Him forever." John Piper

SAVORY BEEF STEW

This hearty soup can be made in large batches and frozen for later meals.

Ingredients:

1 large onion
2 small garlic cloves
16 oz. beef stew meat
2 medium carrots
2 lbs. fresh tomatoes
1 cup water
1 cup all-natural beef broth
1 tsp dried oregano
1 tsp dried basil
1/4 tsp baking soda
Seasoning salt, to taste

Directions:

1. Crush tomatoes in a food processor or blender; adding one cup of water before pureeing.
2. In a large soup pot, heat onion and garlic over medium heat until soft, making sure not to burn garlic.
3. Add beef to pot and heat to brown meat.
4. Dice carrots, add them along with spices to beef mixture.
5. Pour in tomatoes and beef stock and cook for 10 min.
6. Add 1/4 tsp baking soda and stir.
7. Sprinkle with seasoning salt, if desired.
8. Put a lid on the pot and allow to simmer for at least one hour before serving.

"[God] will never fail you or forsake you." Hebrews 13:5

STEAK & SPINACH SALAD
Served with Pomegranate Vinaigrette

Ingredients for salad:

5 oz. baby spinach
1 small yellow onion
1 cup walnuts
1 cup pecans
12 oz. grilled steak

Ingredients for dressing:

1/3 cup pomegranate infused vinegar
1/2 cup olive oil
1/4 cup frozen blueberries
1 tbs dijon mustard
1/2 tsp garlic powder
1/2 tsp pepper
1/8 tsp salt

Directions for salad:

1. Mix veggies and nuts together in a large bowl.
2. Layer strips of steak on top of salad.
3. Top with Pomegranate Vinaigrette

Directions for dressing:

1. In a food processor, mix vinegar, oil, mustard, and spices together until well-combined.
2. Add blueberries and continue processing until smooth.
3. Pour over salad or use as a marinade for your favorite meat.

"God created me—and you—to live with a single, all-embracing, all-transforming passion—namely, a passion to glorify God by enjoying and displaying his supreme excellence in all the spheres of life." John Piper

SPICED FRUIT SALAD

You will be amazed at the flavors created from using only a few simple ingredients!

Ingredients:

1 orange
1 Granny Smith apple, diced
1/3 cup pecans, chopped
1/2 tsp cinnamon
2 tbs honey, optional

Directions:

1. In a small bowl, mix prepared fruit together.
2. Add cinnamon, nuts, and honey and stir until cinnamon mixture is equally distributed.
3. Chill in refrigerator for at least one hour before serving.

Serves 2

The earth is full of the goodness of the Lord." Psalm 33:5

BACON & TOMATO SALAD

With healthy fats and loads of protein, this salad is perfect for any meal of the day.

Ingredients:

1 ripe avocado, cut into chunks
2 hard-boiled eggs, chopped
2-3 roma tomatoes, diced
1/2 lemon, juiced
4 slices of bacon, cooked and crumbled
Salt and pepper, to taste
1/2 tsp garlic powder
Pinch of parsley

Directions:

1. In a medium bowl stir tomatoes, lemon juice, salt, pepper, garlic, and parsley together.
2. Carefully stir in avocado, eggs, and bacon into tomato mixture.
3. Chill and serve.

Serves 2

"[God] loves each one of us like there is only one of us to love." Max Lucado

CHICKEN SALAD
This delicious salad will awe any crowd!

Ingredients:

2 1/2 lbs. frozen chicken breasts
1 small bag of frozen peas, thawed
1 1/2-2lbs. of red grapes, sliced in half
1 cup sliced almonds
1 cup (or more) of Paleo mayo
Seasoning Salt, to taste
Olive oil

Directions:

1. Lightly oil a large baking dish and place chicken inside.
2. Drizzle chicken with olive oil and sprinkle with seasoning salt.
3. Bake at 350 °F for 20 minutes or until fully cooked.
4. Remove from oven and allow to cool for 5 minutes.
5. Cut chicken into bite size pieces and put in a large bowl.
6. Add remaining and gently stir until well combined.
7. Serve chilled.

Serves 6-8

"The steadfast love of the Lord never ceases; his mercies never come to an end; they are new every morning."
Lamentations 3:22-23

SALSA SALAD

This is a perfect base salad to build off of...or leave it as is.

Ingredients:

5-6 tomatillos, cut into small pieces
1 bunch of cilantro, chopped
1 small yellow onion, diced
2 ripe avocados, cut into small pieces
1 large handful of baby spinach
1 lime, squeezed
1 tsp garlic powder
Salt and pepper, to taste

Directions:

1. On a bed of spinach, add all veggies and toss.
2. In a small bowl, mix lime, garlic, salt, and pepper. Pour dressing over salad.

Serves 2

**"Be content with what you have, for God has said, "Never will I leave you; never will I forsake you." So say with confidence, "The Lord is my helper; I will not be afraid."
Hebrews 13:5-6**

RAINBOW KABOBS
A one-dish meal with unbelievable flavor!

Ingredients:

5 lbs. chicken breast, cubed
1 package baby bella mushrooms
1 package bacon, cut into 2-inch strips
2 zucchinis, sliced
4 bell peppers of varied colors
2 carrots, peeled and sliced
2 cups water, for skewer
Wooden Skewers (approximately 40)

Marinade for chicken and veggies:

1 cup olive oil
1/4 cup white balsamic vinegar
1 tbs garlic powder
1 tsp onion powder
1 tsp dried basil
1/2 tsp ground cayenne pepper

Directions:

1. Prepare chicken and veggies and marinate overnight, or for at least 4-6 hours.
2. Before assembling skewers, soak skewers in water for 20 minutes. This prevents skewers from burning when on the grill.
3. Assemble skewers by alternating colors of veggies; adding chicken and bacon evenly throughout.
4. Cook on a grill until chicken is fully cooked, being careful not to overcook.

Serves 6-8

It's exciting to live in complete oneness with the will of God. It is never dull or static because it is not a one-time, once-for-all commitment. It is something we have to work at constantly, moment by moment.
Evelyn Christenson

TURKEY STEW

This hearty stew is perfect for a cold or rainy day!

Ingredients:

1 lb. ground turkey
1 tbs coconut oil, for frying
2 garlic cloves
1 medium onion
4 cups spinach or swiss chard
7 oz. coconut milk
1 1/2 cups chicken broth
1/2 cup roasted red peppers, diced
1 tbs spicy mustard
1 tsp oregano
1 tsp arrowroot powder
Salt and pepper, to taste

Directions:

1. Sauté onions in a large frying pan over medium-high heat. Once tender, add garlic and ground turkey.
2. After meat has browned, add spinach, 1/2 cup chicken broth, peppers, and oregano.
3. Lower heat to medium-low and add milk, arrowroot powder, and remaining chicken broth. Stir until arrowroot is completely dissolved into mixture.
4. Add spicy mustard and simmer for 10 minutes.
5. This dish taste even better the next day!

Serves 4

"Cast your cares upon the Lord, for he cares for you." I Peter 5:7

ENTREES

SAUSAGE ZUCCA
An Italian favorite in our house!

Ingredients:

3 yellow squashes, sliced
3 zucchini squashes, sliced
1 onion, chopped finely
1/2 lb. Italian sausage, sliced
6 slices bacon, cut into small pieces
2 tbs garlic powder
1 tsp dried oregano
2 eggs
1/2 cup baby spinach

Directions:

1. Preheat oven to 350 °F.
2. In a soup pot, cook bacon and sausage together for about 7-10 minutes.
3. Add onion and sauté mixture until sausage begins to brown and bacon becomes crispy.
4. Add squash and stir to blend flavors throughout.
5. Heat until squash becomes tender, moisture from squash is cooked out, and there is little to no liquid in the pot.
6. Salt and pepper, to taste.
7. Remove from heat.
8. Beat eggs in a small bowl, pour over squash mixture and stir completely.
9. Pour into a 9 X 13 baking dish and cook for 30 minutes.

Serves 6

"Whosoever trusts in the Lord, happy is he." Proverbs 16:20

SHRIMP STUFFED CHICKEN

This can be made ahead of time and frozen. Simply reheat and serve!

Ingredients:

2 chicken breasts
1/2 lb. shrimp, peeled and deveined
6 oz. lite coconut milk
2 tbs coconut oil, for pan
1/2 cup almond flour
2 lemons, juiced
1/2 medium yellow onion
4-5 roma tomatoes
1/4 green bell pepper
1 tsp dried parsley
2 cloves of garlic, minced
1/2 tsp ground cayenne pepper
1/2 tsp oregano
1 tsp paprika
2 tsp arrowroot powder
Salt and pepper, to taste
1/4 tsp garlic powder
1/8 tsp seasoning salt

Directions:

1. Preheat oven to 350°F.
2. Heat skillet with oil over medium-low heat.
3. Add shrimp and sprinkle tops with garlic powder; cook for 2-4 minutes, flipping once. Remove from pan when pink.
4. Add milk and tomatoes to pan and simmer until tomatoes are tender.
5. Add veggies and spices and continue cooking until veggies are tender.
6. Stir in arrowroot powder. Continue stirring until all lumps are gone.
7. Cut cooked shrimp into small pieces and return to pan. Stir in half of lemon juice.
8. Grease a 9x13 pan with coconut oil.
9. Butterfly chicken breasts and spoon shrimp mixture inside. Roll chicken to enclose mixture.
10. Place chicken in dish and sprinkle with almond flour, remaining lemon juice, and seasoning salt.
11. Bake for 30 min.

Serves 2

"In Your [God's] presence is fullness of Joy!" Psalm 16:11

MARINATED RIBS

A tangy twist to an all-time favorite!

Ingredients :

2 lbs. beef short ribs
1 1/4 cup blueberries
1/3 mango
1/2 onion chopped
2-3 garlic cloves, minced
1/4 cup apple cider vinegar
1/2 cup olive oil
1/2 tsp chili powder
2 stalks scallions, chopped
1/2 tsp seasoning salt
1/4 tsp ground ginger

Directions:

1. In a blender, blend all ingredients except ribs to create a marinade.
2. Pour marinade over ribs and keep in refrigerate for at least 4 hours (over night is best).
3. Grill or broil ribs until done (time depends on how you like your ribs)

Serves 2

"O satisfy us in the morning with Your lovingkindness,
That we may sing for joy and be glad all our days." Psalm 90:14

BLACKENED WHOLE CHICKEN

This easy and rich tasting recipe will satisfy any small crowd!

Ingredients :

1 whole chicken
1 tbs paprika
1 tsp cayenne pepper
2 tsp garlic powder
1 tsp onion powder
1 tsp black pepper
1 tsp dried thyme
1/2 tsp dried oregano
1 tsp seasoning salt
4 tbs olive oil
1 lemon, juiced
1 garlic clove, minced

Directions:

1. Preheat oven to 350°F.
2. In a small bowl mix all ingredients except chicken and 1 tbs oil.
3. In a roasting pan, grease pan with 1 tbs oil.
4. Remove innards from chicken and rinse inside and outside of chicken with cold water.
5. Pour seasoning mixture over entire chicken.
6. Bake for 2 hrs, or until fully cooked.

Serves 4-6

"On the whole, God's love for us is a much safer subject to think about than our love for him. No one can always have devout feelings.... But the great thing to remember is that, though our feelings come and go, his love for us does not." C.S. Lewis

GARLIC PULLED PORK

This abundant dish is perfect for parties or big eaters!

Ingredients :

3-4 lbs. pork, shoulder cut
1 can tomato paste (or 4-6 roma tomatoes cooked to a paste)
1/4 cup xylitol or honey
1/4 cup apple cider vinegar
1-2 tbs seasoning salt
1 tsp black pepper
1-2 tbs garlic powder
1 lime, juiced
1 onion, chopped
1 tsp chili powder
1/2 cup water

Directions:

1. In a medium bowl, mix together all ingredients except pork and water.
2. Put pork in a large crock pot and add liquid mixture.
3. Add 1/2 cup water.
4. Put lid on crock pot. Cook on high for 6 hours; stirring occasionally.
5. Once fully cooked, pull pork apart using two forks.

Serves 10-12

"Heaven is a place of unparalleled and indescribable joy."   John Piper

CILANTRO PESTO CHICKEN
This bold tasting pesto tastes great on meat, veggies, and is even wonderful as a dip!

Ingredients :

3 lbs. chicken tenderloins
4 tbs olive oil
2 tbs white balsamic vinegar
1 tsp garlic powder
1/2 tsp ginger
1/2 tsp seasoning salt

Ingredients for pesto:

1 bunch of cilantro, use only the leaves
2 large garlic cloves, minced
1/4 tsp powdered ginger
1/4 cup olive oil
1/4 cup almond butter
1 tsp honey
3/4 cup unsweetened vanilla almond milk
1/4 tsp seasoning salt
1/2 cup chicken broth removed from pan after cooking chicken
1 tbs arrowroot powder

Directions:

1. Preheat oven to 350°F.
2. Pour 3 tbs oil into a 9x13 casserole dish.
3. Add chicken and drizzle with vinegar and remaining oil.
4. Sprinkle chicken with spices and cook for 20 minutes or until fully cooked.
5. While chicken is baking, begin making pesto.
6. In a blender, blend all ingredients together except chicken broth and arrowroot powder.
7. After chicken is done cooking, remove 1/2 cup broth from pan.
8. In a small sauce pan add pesto, broth, and arrowroot powder. Cook over medium-low heat, stirring constantly
9. Pour pesto over meat and serve.

Serves 4-6

"True joy comes only from God and He shares this joy with those who walk in fellowship with Him."
Jerry Bridges

BURGER BITES

These scrumptious bites are a perfect make-and-take food!

Ingredients :

1 lb. ground beef
1 tbs coconut oil
1 tsp garlic powder
1/4 tsp onion powder
1 small yellow onion, chopped finely
4 roma tomatoes, sliced
1/3 cup chopped dill pickles
2 tbs Nutiva ® Coconut Manna
2 tbs spicy mustard
6 large eggs
1/2 cup almond flour
24 cupcake liners

Directions:

1. Preheat oven to 350°F.
2. In a large skillet heat coconut oil over medium heat.
3. Add beef and sprinkle with garlic powder and onion powder.
4. Mix remaining ingredients in a medium bowl.
5. Line 2 cupcake pans with paper liners.
6. Spray each liner with coconut oil.
7. Place one slice of tomato on the bottom of each cup.
8. Divide 1/2 of the egg mixture evenly between all the cups and add the browned beef.
9. Top each cup with remainder of the egg mixture.
10. Bake for 25-30 minutes.

The God who created, names, and numbers the stars in the heavens also numbers the hairs of my head. He pays attention to very big things and to very small ones. What matters to me matters to Him, and that changes my life." Elisabeth Elliot

NUT-BREADED CHICKEN
Better than breaded chicken but with more protein and far fewer carbs!

Ingredients :

4 chicken breasts
4 cups almond meal
2 eggs
3 tbs almond milk, unsweetened vanilla
1 tsp seasoning salt
1 tsp onion powder
1 tsp garlic powder
1 tsp paprika
1 dash of celery seed
3-4 tbs olive oil

Directions:

1. Preheat oven to 350 °F.
2. Pour oil in a 9x13 casserole dish.
3. In a large bowl, mix almond meal and spices.
4. In a medium bowl, beat eggs with oil and milk.
5. Rinse chicken breasts in cold water and dip in egg mixture.
6. Roll chicken into almond flour mixture making sure all sides are covered.
7. Place battered chicken in casserole dish and bake for 30 minutes, or until fully cooked.

Serves 4

"Remember, you have one life. That's all. You were made for God. Don't waste it." John Piper

SPICY PORK CHOPS

This breading is also great on chicken and fish!

Ingredients :

4 Pork Chops *thin sliced*
6 tbs olive oil
1/2 cup almond flour *use more, about 1 cup*
1 tsp cayenne pepper *use less*
1/2 tsp seasoning salt
1 tbs olive oil, for pan

Directions:

1. Mix olive oil and cayenne pepper *and seasoning salt* in a bowl.
2. Dip pork chops in oil and flour both sides with almond flour.
3. Heat 1 tbs olive oil over medium-high heat in a pan.
4. Fry pork chops on both sides until crispy.

Serves 4

"Being confident of this, that he who began a good work in you will carry it on to completion until the day of Christ Jesus." Philippians 1:6

GREEK PORK CHOPS

Pull out your favorite toga and fork and get ready for a party in your mouth!

Ingredients:

1 lb. pork chops or tenderloin
1 red pepper, finely chopped
2 garlic cloves, minced
1 1/2 cups baby spinach
1/4 cup pecans, chopped
1/4 cup Kalamata olives, pitted
1-2 tbs olive oil for sautéing
Seasoning salt, to taste

Directions:
1. Preheat oven to 350°F.
2. In a medium frying pan, sauté red peppers in oil and garlic.
3. Add spinach and cook until spinach is wilted. Remove from heat.
4. Butterfly pork and flatten meat with a meat tenderizer. Once meat is thin, add veggies evenly.
5. Spread nuts and olives on top of veggies and roll meat into a roll.
6. Place rolls close enough together in an oiled 9 X 13 pan to ensure that rolls do not unroll. If you find that rolls do not stay together, use tooth picks to help them stay rolled.
7. Bake for 45-55 minutes, or until meat is fully cooked.

Serves 4

"Being confident of this, that he who began a good work in you will carry it on to completion until the day of Christ Jesus." Philippians 1:6

GRILLED WHOLE CHICKEN
Packed with flavor and surprisingly low on ingredients!

Ingredients :

1 whole chicken
3 tbs olive oil
2-3 tbs poultry seasoning
2 tsb seasoning salt

Directions:

1. Heat grill or preheat oven to 350°F.
2. Remove insides of chicken, if necessary.
3. Rinse, and rub oil over entire chicken.
4. Liberally sprinkle poultry seasoning and seasoning salt on outside and inside of chicken.
5. Grill for 30-45 minutes or until completely cooked (internal temperature of 165°F), turning occasionally. Or, bake in an oven for 1 1/2 hrs, or until fully cooked.

Serves 4-6

The greatest privilege God gives to you is the freedom to approach Him at any time. You are not only authorized to speak to Him; you are invited. You are not only permitted; you are expected. God waits for you to communicate with Him. You have instant, direct access to God. God loves mankind so much, and in a very special sense His children, that He has made Himself available to you at all times." Wesley L. Duewel

CHICKEN A LA NANCY

Bursting with flavor!!

Ingredients :

4 chicken breasts, cubed
1/4 cup olive oil
1 garlic clove, minced
8 oz. baby bella mushrooms, sliced
1 lemon, sliced thin
1/2 cup chicken broth
1/2 tsp oregano
1/4 tsp pepper
1 tbs arrowroot powder
10-12 oz bag frozen artichokes

Directions:

1. In a large frying pan, heat oil over medium-high heat. Add chicken and cook for 5-7 minutes, or until fully cooked; turning once. Remove chicken from pan.
2. Add garlic, mushrooms, and lemon and cook until tender.
3. Add arrowroot powder and stir until completely dissolved.
4. Sprinkle all spices evenly into pan and stir.
5. Add broth and bring to boil. Stir constantly until sauce thickens.
6. Add artichokes and cooked chicken and simmer for 3-5 minutes.

Serves 4

"No joy on earth is equal to the bliss of being taken up with love to Christ." Charles Spurgeon

CHICKEN CLAFOUTI

This hearty recipe can be made ahead and frozen. Simply reheat and enjoy!

Ingredients :

1 Perfect Pie Crust, Pg. 90
6 eggs
6 tbs Nutiva ® Coconut Manna
3/4 cup coconut milk
4 cups cooked chicken breast, shredded
2 tbs dried onion
1 1/2 tsp garlic powder
1/2 tsp oregano
1 cup fresh spinach, chopped

Directions:

1. Preheat oven to 400 °F.
2. Prepare pie crust in a deep dish pie pan.
3. Whisk eggs, coconut manna and milk together in a large bowl.
4. Add chicken, spinach, and spices to egg mixture and pour into prepared pie shell.
5. Bake for 45 minutes, or until top is lightly browned.

Serves 8

God is not an elusive dream or a phantom to chase, but a divine person to know. He does not avoid us, but seeks us. When we seek Him, the contact is instantaneous." Neva Coyle

CHICKEN LETTUCE WRAPS
A tasty dish perfect for home or on-the-go!

Ingredients :

2 cooked chicken breasts (seasoned with seasoning salt)
2 ripe avocados
4 roma tomatoes
1 small jalapeno pepper, deseeded and diced
1/4 small yellow onion, diced
3 garlic cloves, minced
1/4 cup fresh cilantro, chopped
1 lime, juiced
6-8 large romaine lettuce leaves

Directions:

1. In a medium bowl, mash avocados and mix in all ingredients, except lettuce.
2. Spoon mixture onto lettuce leaves and wrap leaves to hold mixture.
3. Serve with your favorite dressing or sauce.

Serves 2

"The best cure for loneliness is developing an intimate relationship with Jesus Christ."
Anonymous

SHEPHERD'S PIE
Incredibly tasty and bursting with depths of flavor!

Ingredients :

1 lb. ground grass-fed beef or ground turkey
1 head cauliflower
2-4 tbs olive oil
1 tsp garlic powder
Salt and pepper, to taste
1 medium yellow onion, chopped
1 cup frozen peas and carrots
3/4 cup frozen green beans
1 tbs arrowroot powder
3/4 cup beef broth
1 tbs fresh rosemary
1 tsp dried thyme
Seasoning salt, to taste

Directions:

1. Preheat oven to 400 °F.
2. Steam cauliflower until tender and puree in food processor. Salt with seasoning salt and set aside.
3. Heat oil in a large frying pan and sauté onions until soft. Add ground beef/turkey, peas, and carrots and cook until meat is browned.
4. Sprinkle arrowroot powder evenly over skillet and stir until well-combined.
5. Add broth and herbs and simmer on low for 3-5 minutes, stirring often. Salt and pepper to desired taste.
6. Pour into a deep dish pie pan and spread cauliflower puree over top.
7. Bake for 30-40 minutes.

Serves 6

"There is not in the world a kind of life more sweet and delightful than that of a continual conversation with God." Brother Lawrence

MUSHROOM & PEPPER CHICKEN
Infused with hearty, deep flavors!

Ingredients :

1 lb. chicken breasts, cubed
10 oz. baby bella mushrooms
1 medium onion, cut into thin strips
2 cups mixed bell peppers (can be frozen), diced
7 oz. lite coconut milk
1 garlic clove, minced
1/2 cup olive oil
Seasoning salt and pepper, to taste

Directions:

1. In a large bowl, mix oil (all except 2 tbs), garlic, seasoning salt, and pepper. Add chicken and mix.
2. Allow chicken to marinate for at least one hour.
3. Sauté onions, mushrooms, and peppers over medium-high heat until tender.
4. Add coconut milk and cook for an additional 5 minutes stirring often.
5. Lower heat to simmer.
6. In a separate pan, heat 2 tbs olive oil over medium-high heat. Add chicken and cook until done.
7. Add chicken to veggie mix and serve immediately.

Serves 2

"Open your hearts to the love God instills... God loves you tenderly. What He gives you is not to be kept under lock and key but to be shared." Mother Teresa

VIVA ITALIA MEATBALLS

Finally, a healthy meatball with true Italian goodness!! My grandmother would be proud!

Ingredients :

1 lb. ground beef
1 lb. (real) Italian sausage, removed from casing
2 garlic cloves, minced
1 sprig rosemary, fresh and minced
1/4 tsp dried thyme
1/4 tsp dried oregano
1 tsp dried onion
1/2 cup almond meal
2 eggs, beaten
1 tbs olive oil

Directions:

1. In a large bowl, mix all ingredients together until well combined.
2. Roll meatballs into 1 1/2 -inch balls.
3. Heat oil in a large pan. Once oil is fully heated, add meatballs.
4. Fry meatballs until browned, turning often.

Serves 6

"Let God's promises shine on your problems." Corrie Ten Boom

SPICED ISLAND CHICKEN

The unique blend of flavors in this dish is sure to satisfy!

Ingredients :

4 large chicken breasts
1 (8 oz) can crushed pineapple (or 1/2 cup fresh)
1 lb. pureed peaches
1 cup orange juice
1/2 cup raisins
1/2 cup almonds, sliced
1/4 tsp cinnamon
1/4 tsp ground cloves
Pepper, to taste
Seasoning salt

Directions:

1. In a large pan, simmer chicken, pineapple, orange juice, raisins, almonds, cinnamon, and cloves for 45- 50 minutes.
2. Add peach puree and simmer for an additional 20 minutes while sauce thickens.
3. Pepper to taste.

Serves 4

There are four ways God answers prayer: 1) No, not yet; 2) No, I love you too much; 3) Yes, I thought you'd never ask; 4) Yes, and here's more." Anne Lewis

ITALIAN ROAST BEEF
The best roast beef recipe you will ever try!

Ingredients :

4 lbs. bottom round roast
2 large onions, sliced
3 garlic cloves, minced
1 tbs garlic powder
1 tbs dried oregano
16 oz bag of carrots, sliced
2 tbs olive oil

Directions:

1. In a large skillet, heat oil and sear all sides of roast.
2. Add roast and remaining ingredients into a large crock pot and fill with water.
3. Cook on high for 6-8 hours, or until meat easliy falls apart with a fork.

Serves 8

"God wants to speak to us more than we want to listen. He is a God of love, and love longs to communicate." Linda Schubert

APPLE PORK CHOPS
Best if prepared the night before so flavors can marinade.

Ingredients :

1 lb. pork chops
1/3 cup pecans, chopped
1 egg, beaten
1 garlic clove, minced
2 tsp olive oil
1/4 cup green onions, chopped
1 apple, chopped
Salt and pepper, to taste

Directions:

1. In a medium bowl mix pecans, garlic, green onions, and apple.
2. Pound pork chops with a meat tenderizer.
3. Dip pork chops in beaten eggs and coat in pecan mixture.
4. Pan fry until fully cooked, flipping once.
5. Place meat in a 9 X 13 baking dish and refrigerate overnight.
6. Reheat the following day at 350 °F for 20 minutes.

Serves 4

"To fall in love with God is the greatest of all romances; To seek Him, the greatest adventure; To find him, the greatest human achievement." Augustine

STUFFED FISH
Light and full of flavor!

Ingredients:

2 lbs. tilapia
1 lemon, juiced
1/4 cup olive oil
1 tsp cayenne pepper
1 tsp cumin
1/3 cup almonds, ground
4 tsp olive oil
3 tbs dried parsley
3 garlic cloves, minced
1/8 tsp allspice

Directions:

1. Preheat oven to 350 °F.
2. In a shallow dish, marinade fish in lemon juice for 20-30 minutes.
3. Remove fish from lemon juice and brush with 2 tbs oil.
4. Sprinkle fish with cayenne pepper and cumin.
5. Sauté nuts in oil until lightly browned.
6. In a small bowl, mix nuts, parsley, garlic, and allspice.
7. Scoop an equal amount of nut mixture onto each fillet and roll fish, securing with toothpicks.
8. Cover dish with foil.
9. Bake for 35 minutes, or until fully cooked.

Serves 4

When God is involved, anything can happen. Be open. Stay that way. God has a beautiful way of bringing good vibrations out of broken chords." Charles Swindoll

SEASONED SALMON
If you are not a salmon-lover, this recipe will turn you into one!

Ingredients :

1 lb. wild salmon
4 roma tomatoes
1 medium shallot, minced
2 garlic cloves, minced
1/2 cup olive oil
1/8 tsp oregano
1 lemon, juiced
1 tsp almond meal
Salt and pepper, to taste

Directions:

1. Preheat oven to 350°F.
2. Use 2 tbs oil to grease a 9 X 13 baking dish and place fish inside.
3. Salt and pepper salmon.
4. In a frying pan heat remaining oil and sauté tomatoes, shallots, garlic, oregano, and lemon juice.
5. Add almond meal and simmer until sauce thickens.
6. Pour sauce over salmon and bake for 10-15 minutes.

Serves 2

"God walks us. He scoops us up in His arms or simply sits with us in silent strength until we cannot avoid the awesome recognition that yes, even now, He is there." Gloria Gaither

CREAMY PESTO PASTA

The versatility and pure flavor of spaghetti squash will help you forget your days of grain pasta!

Ingredients :

1 large spaghetti squash
1 1/2 cups fresh basil leaves
1/2 cup olive oil
2-3 garlic cloves, minced
1/2 cup almonds
1/8 tsp parsley
1/4 cup unsweetened plain almond milk
1/2 cup almond flour

Directions:

1. Preheat oven to 400 °F.
2. Split squash lengthwise and remove seeds.
3. Bake squash face down for 30-45 minutes.
4. In a food processor blend all remaining ingredients, to make pesto.
5. Once squash is fully cooked, remove "pasta" (inside of squash) with a fork.
6. Pour creamy pesto over "pasta".
7. Serve immediately.

Serves 4-6

"Seek to cultivate a buoyant, joyous sense of the crowded kindnesses of God in your daily life."
Alexander MacLaren

COCONUT CHICKEN
Simple, yet full of flavor!

Ingredients :

1 lb. chicken breast
1 egg
1/2 cup almond flour
1/2 cup shredded coconut
Seasoning salt, to taste
2 tbs olive oil

Directions:

1. Preheat oven to 400 °F.
2. In a medium bowl, mix together almond flour and coconut.
3. Beat egg in a small bowl and dip chicken inside, making sure all sides are fully coated.
4. Roll chicken in almond mixture and sprinkle with seasoning salt.
5. Place chicken in a greased pan and bake for 25-35 minutes, or until fully cooked.

Serves 4

"You don't have to be alone in your hurt! Comfort is yours. Joy is an option. And it's all been made possible by your Saviour. He went without comfort so you might have it. He postponed joy so you might share in it. He willingly chose isolation so you might never be alone in your hurt and sorrow." Joni Eareckson Tada

PIZZA

It's movie night and this pizza is a perfect crowd-pleaser!

Ingredients:

3 tsp olive oil
1 cup almond flour
3 tbs cashew butter
1/3 cup egg whites
2 medium very ripe tomatoes, sliced
1/8 cup chopped yellow onions, chopped
1/2 tsp garlic powder
1/8 tsp oregano
Pinch of dried basil
2 large Italian sausages, sliced into 1/2 inch slices
1/4 cup fresh spinach

Directions:

1. Preheat oven to 350 °F.
2. For pizza dough, mix almond flour, cashew butter, and egg whites in a small bowl.
3. Brush a baking stone or baking sheet with olive oil. Spread pizza dough to 1/4" in thickness and top with 1/4 tsp powdered garlic.
4. In a skillet, cook sausage. Keep grease for sauce.
5. Using the same skillet, sauté tomatoes, onions, and garlic in sausage grease.
6. Add oregano and basil and cook until sauce thickens to desired consistency.
7. Spoon sauce onto pizza dough.
8. Top with spinach and sausage.
9. Bake for 15-20 minutes.

Serves 2

"Happy is the person who not only sings, but feels God's eye is on the sparrow, and knows He watches over me. To be simply ensconced in God is true joy." C.C. Colton

ITALIAN CHICKEN THIGHS

You'll think you were in Italy! No joke, these are DELISH!

Ingredients:

1/2 lb. Italian sausage
2 lbs. chicken thighs
1/4 tsp pepper
2 garlic cloves, minced
1/2 tsp rosemary
3/4 cup chicken broth
1/8 tsp onion powder
1/8 tsp garlic powder

Directions:

1. Cook sausage in a large skillet over medium heat.
2. Degrease sausage on a paper towel-covered plate and add chicken thighs to skillet (do not remove sausage grease from skillet).
3. Sprinkle chicken with pepper and continue to cook until thighs are browned.
4. Remove chicken from skillet.
5. Add onion to pan and cook until tender.
6. Stir garlic and rosemary into pan and cook for 5 minutes.
7. Cut sausage into 1/2-inch long pieces.
8. Pour broth into pan and add sausage and chicken back into the pan.
9. Simmer, covered, for 30 minutes.

Serves 6

"[The LORD said, 'I have loved you with an everlasting love; therefore I have drawn you with lovingkindness.'" Jeremiah 31:3

SIDE DISHES

"BREADED" ZUCCHINI
A tasty side that even your children will love!

Ingredients:

4-6 small zucchinis
3 large eggs, beaten
1 1/2 cups almond flour
1 tsp garlic powder
1 tsp onion powder
1/2 tsp paprika
1 tsp oregano
1/2 tsp salt, if desired
1/2 tsp pepper

Directions:

1. Preheat oven to 350 °F.
2. Mix all dry ingredients except zucchini in a large bowl.
3. Peel zucchini; dip in eggs.
4. Pour dry mixture onto a large plate.
5. After dipping zucchini in eggs, coat with dry mixture and place in an olive oil-greased 9 X 13 pan.
6. Bake for 20-30 minutes, or until lightly browned.

Serves 6

Joy is not the absence of suffering. It is the presence of God. " Anonymous

GARLIC GREEN BEANS
A must-have recipe when making green beans!

Ingredients:

1 lb. green beans, cut
1/2 small yellow onion, diced
2-4 tbs olive oil
2-3 large garlic cloves
1 cup almond slices

Directions:

1. Sauté onions in oil until soft.
2. Add garlic and green beans, cooking until green beans are tender.
3. Pour almond slices into skillet and cook for an additional 10-12 minutes.

Serves 4-6

"The most valuable thing the Psalms do for me is to express the same delight in God which made David dance." C.S. Lewis

ITALIAN ZUCCHINI
Quick, easy, and bursting with flavor!

Ingredients:

4-6 small zucchinis
2-3 tbs olive oil
1/2 tsp garlic powder
1/4 tsp onion powder
Oregano, to taste

Directions:

1. Slice zucchini thinly long-wise and lay in 9x13 dish drizzled with 1-2 tbs olive oil.
2. Pour remaining olive oil over zucchini.
3. Sprinkle tops with garlic, onion, and oregano.
4. Bake at 350 for 20-30 minutes.

Serves 6

"A tongue filled with laughter and praise is a reflection of a heart filled to overflowing with the joy of the Lord. What a joy it is just to be with someone whose heart is full." M. Hoskins

BEEF SUSHI
Better known as umami, this dish brings the tastes of the East right to your table!

Ingredients:

Nori seaweed sheets
1/2 lb. roast beef
1/2 of an avocado
1 carrot, thinly sliced
Cucumbers, thinly sliced
Paleo Mayo

Paleo Mayo ingredients:

1/4 tsp mustard
1/4 tsp salt, optional
1/4 tsp paprika
1/8 tsp ground red pepper
2 egg yolks
2 tbs white balsamic vinegar
2 cups grape seed or coconut oil

Directions:

1. Using a sushi mat (or a stiff kitchen towel), lay seaweed shiny-side down.
2. Layer meat, avocado, cucumbers, and carrots on seaweed.
3. Spread a thin layer of Paleo Mayo over all.
4. Tightly roll seaweed and slice into desired sushi sizes.

Mayo recipe:
1. Combine all ingredients except oil in a food processor.
2. Pulse to combine all ingredients.
3. Gradually add oil while keeping processor on.
4. When mayo begins to whiten, stop processor and scrape sides. Turn processor on for 20-30 more seconds.
5. Keeps in refrigerator for up to 3 weeks.

Serves 6

"We are like those who dream. Our mouths are filled with laughter, our tongues with songs of joy. It is said among the nations, 'The LORD has done great things for them.' Yes, the LORD has done great things for us, and we are filled with joy." Psalm 126:2-3

2-TONED CARROTS
Top with Cilantro Pesto for an impressive side.

Ingredients:

1 lb. yellow and orange carrots (or orange only)
1/2 cup Cilantro Pesto, Pg. 50
1 tsp oil
1/4 cup chicken broth
1/2 tsp seasoning salt
1 tsp oil (preferably coconut oil)

Directions:

1. Heat carrots over medium heat with 1 tsp oil or coconut until tender.
2. Add pesto and cook for 10 minutes.
3. Add chicken broth and seasoning salt and cook for an additional 5-10 minutes.

Serves 4

"The Lord is kind. He is good to all who take refuge under his wings."　John Piper

HERB BREAD

Serve with your favorite soup or salad, or use to make your favorite sandwich!

Ingredients:

1 cup almond flour
1 cup arrowroot flour
1 tsp garlic powder
1/2 dried parsley
1 tsp dried rosemary
1 tsp onion powder
1/2 tsp dried oregano
1 egg
1/8 cup honey
1/8 cup almond milk, unsweetened
1/4 tsp baking soda
1/4 tsp baking powder

Directions:

1. Preheat oven to 350°F.
2. Mix all wet ingredients in a small bowl and set aside.
3. In a large bowl, combine all dry ingredients together.
4. Stir in wet ingredients and roll into a ball.
5. Place dough in a greased bread pan, flattening to form a loaf, and bake for 30 minutes.

Serves 4-6

"To be filled with God is to be filled with joy." Anonymous

GARLIC PARSNIP FRIES
A delicious way to eat your veggies!

Ingredients:

3 medium parsnips
3 tbs almond butter
2 tbs coconut or olive oil
1/4 tsp seasoning salt
1/2 tsp garlic powder
1/2 cup unsweetened coconut flakes

Directions:

1. Preheat oven to 400°F.
2. Wash, peel, and slice parsnips lengthwise.
3. In a medium bowl, mix together almond butter, oil, salt, and garlic.
4. Toss parsnips in almond butter mixture and roll in coconut flakes.
5. Bake on a baking sheet for 45-50 minutes, or until golden brown.

Serves 4-6

"Whence comes this idea that if what we are doing is fun, it can't be God's will? The God who made giraffes, a baby's fingernails, a puppy's tail, a crook necked squash, the bobwhite's call, and a young girl's giggle, has a sense of humor. Make no mistake about that." Catherine Marshall

HOT CHICKEN & BACON BITES
Tasty poppers filled with spicy kick!

Ingredients:

1 large chicken breast, cut into 1 inch cubes
4-6 hot peppers of your choice (we use pepperoncinis), sliced thin
4 strips of bacon
Seasoning salt
Olive oil
Toothpicks

Directions:

1. Sprinkle chicken with seasoning salt.
2. Place 1-2 slices of pepper on each piece of chicken and wrap with 1/2 a piece of bacon.
3. Secure bacon with a toothpick and heat in a skillet with olive oil.
4. Cook over medium heat for 8-10 minutes or until chicken is fully cooked and bacon is crispy.

Serves 4

**"It is pleasing to God whenever thou rejoicest or laughest from the bottom of thy heart."
Martin Luther**

SWEET POTATO FRIES

Can be prepared ahead of time and frozen until ready to bake.

Ingredients:

5-6 medium sweet potatoes, peeled and sliced into 1/4 inch wide strips
1 tsp seasoning salt
1/2 tsp paprika
1/8 cup olive oil

Directions:

1. Preheat oven to 450°F.
2. In a large bowl mix oil and seasonings until well combined.
3. Add potatoes and toss until potatoes are completely covered with oil mixture.
4. Place potatoes on a baking sheet and bake for about 20 minutes or until golden brown. Turn potatoes occasionally.
5. Cool for 5 minutes before serving.

Serves 8

God gives out Wisdom free, and is plainspoken in Knowledge and Understanding. He's a rich mine of Common Sense for those who live well, a personal bodyguard to the candid and sincere. He keeps his eye on all who live honestly, and pays special attention to his loyally committed ones. Proverbs 2:6-8

NO POTATO SALAD
Same great flavor, but without the heavy carbs.

Ingredients:

1 head of cauliflower, cut into 1/2 inch pieces
3 hard boiled eggs, peeled and cut into small pieces
1/2-1 tsp garlic powder
1/2 tsp onion flakes
2 tsp spicy mustard
2-4 tbs Paleo mayo
2 lemons, squeezed
Salt and pepper, to taste

Directions:

1. Steam cauliflower until al dente and allow to cool.
2. Place in a large bowl and add remaining ingredients.
3. Mix gently and serve chilled.

Serves 6-8

"And God is able to bless you abundantly, so that in all things at all times, having all that you need, you will abound in every good work." 2 Corinthians 9:8

STUFFED PORTOBELLAS

Make as a side or as a meal.

Ingredients:

1 container of baby bella mushroom caps
6 oz. of Albacore tuna, in water
1/2 large avocado
1/8-1/4 tsp garlic powder
Pinch of cayenne pepper
Salt and pepper to taste

Directions:

1. Sprinkle both sides of mushroom caps with garlic and grill in a medium-sized skillet.
2. Mix all remaining ingredients together in a small bowl, and spread on grilled caps.

Serves 6

"Take delight in the LORD, and he will give you the desires of your heart." Psalm 37:4

ZUCCHINI CHIPS

Way better than potato chips! Go ahead and eat a handful... guilt-free!

Ingredients:

1 large zucchini, sliced into 1/8 inch slices
Seasoning salt, to taste
Onion powder, optional

Directions:

1. Sprinkle zucchini with salt and onion powder.
2. Dry in a food dehydrator for 5 1/2 hours at 130°F., or until dry and crispy.

Serves 2

"Do not limit the limitless God! With Him, face the future unafraid because you are never alone."
Mrs. Charles E Cowman

DEVILED GUACAMOLE EGGS
A perfect finger food.

Ingredients:

3 hard-boiled eggs, peeled and halved
1 ripe avocado, mashed
1 tsp hot sauce
1 lime, juiced
Garlic powder, to taste
Onion powder, to taste
Salt and pepper, optional

Directions:

1. Remove yolks from eggs and mash in a small bowl.
2. Add avocado, hot sauce, lime juice, and spices.
3. Spoon into egg white halves and serve.

Serves 2-4

"The life of faith is a daily exploration of the constant and countless ways in which God's grace and love are experienced." Eugene Peterson

DESSERTS

RASPBERRY PECAN TRUFFLES
A perfect party treat.

Ingredients:

1/2 cup raw almond butter
2 tbs Polaner® All-fruit jelly
1 tbs honey
1 tbs maple syrup
2 cups dark chocolate chips
1/4 cup almond milk, unsweetened vanilla
3/4 cup crushed pecans

Directions:

1. Put 1 cup chocolate, almond butter, spreadable fruit, honey, syrup, and milk in a small saucepan and cook on low until all ingredients are melted.
2. Refrigerate for one hour.
3. Remove chocolate mixture from refrigerator and roll into small balls.
4. Roll balls in pecans.
5. Melt remaining cup of chocolate.
6. Dip pecan balls into melted chocolate and place on parchment paper until cooled.
7. Refrigerate for at least one hour.
8. Serve!

Serves 8-10

"We aren't just thrown on this earth like dice tossed across a table. We are lovingly placed here for a purpose." Charles Swindoll

PERFECT PIE CRUST
Double-crust recipe

Ingredients:

2 1/2 cups almond flour
1/2 cup coconut oil
1/4 cup Nutiva ® Coconut Manna
1/4 cup sea salt, optional
1/3 cup water

Directions:

1. Pour flour into a large bowl.
2. Add all ingredients, mixing after each addition.
3. Roll dough into 2 balls and store in the refrigerator until ready to bake.

"Desire that your life count for something great! Long for your life to have eternal significance. Want this! Don't coast through life without a passion." John Piper

MACAROONS
A light cookie that is not super sweet.

Ingredients:

1 7oz bag of shredded coconut, unsweetened
1 cup raw almonds
1/4 cup honey
4 large egg whites
1 tsp vanilla
1/2 tsp cinnamon

Directions:

1. Preheat oven to 325°F.
2. In a large bowl, mix all ingredients together.
3. Drop mixture onto a greased baking sheet.
4. Bake for 20-25 minutes, or until golden brown.

Serves 6-8

"God is most glorified in us when we are most satisfied in Him". John Piper

CHOCOLATE PROTEIN FUDGE

Perfect reward after a good workout! Don't worry these are healthy, too!

Ingredients:

3/4 cup coconut milk
1/4 cup Nutiva ® Coconut Manna
1/4 cup raw almond butter
4 oz. unsweetened dark baker's chocolate
1/2 tsp vanilla
1/2 cup maple syrup
1/2 cup dried fruit (optional)

Directions:

1. Heat all ingredients on low in a saucepan until all ingredients are liquid. Stir constantly to avoid burning.
2. Cook for five to seven minutes and remove pan from burner.
3. Allow fudge to cool for 10 minutes and pour into a 9 X 9 glass dish.
4. Refrigerate until fudge is solid and cut into 1-inch size squares.
5. Refrigerate leftovers.

Serves 10-15

Though our feelings come and go, God's love for us does not." C.S. Lewis

DARK CHOCOLATE PIE
Delicious doesn't even begin to describe the sheer goodness of this pie!

Ingredients for crust:

1 1/2 cups prunes, or raisins
1 cup pecans, chopped
1/2 cup unsweetened coconut

Ingredients for filling:

3 tbs Nutiva ® Coconut Manna
1/2 cup unsweetened dark cocoa powder
3 small avocados
2 1/2 tbs coconut milk
5 tbs pure maple syrup
1 tsp vanilla extract

Directions:

1. In a food processor, mix prunes and pecans until evenly blended.
2. Add coconut and continue mixing until well combined.
3. Press mixture into a 9" pie pan and bake for 3-5 minutes at 350° F.
4. For filling, in a small saucepan over medium low heat, melt coconut oil and slowly stir in cocoa powder. Spoon into a medium bowl.
5. In a food processor, puree avocados and add to cocoa mixture.
6. Pour coconut milk, maple syrup, and vanilla into bowl and stir until completely combined with cocoa mixture.
7. Pour into pie crust and chill for at least one hour before serving.

Serves 8

"It is only the love of God, disclosed and enacted in Christ, that redeems the human tragedy and makes it tolerable. No, more than tolerable. Wonderful." Mark Twain

KOLACHE

Serve with your favorite hot drink.

Ingredients:

1 Perfect Pie Crust (Pg. 90), uncooked
1 1/2 cups walnuts, crushed
1/3 cup honey
2 tbs Nutiva ® Coconut Manna
4 tbs coconut milk
1 tsp cinnamon

Directions:

1. Preheat oven to 350°F.
2. In a medium bowl, mix all ingredients, except pie crust.
3. Roll pie crust into a large rectangle
4. Liberally spoon filling in center of dough and roll dough so nut mixture is spiraled inside like a pinwheel.
5. Bake on a greased baking sheet for 20 minutes, or until slightly browned on top.
6. Allow to cool for 15-20 minutes and cut in 2-inch thick pieces.

Serves 6-8

"You are valuable because you exist. Not because of what you do or what you have done, but simply because you are." Max Lucado

CHOCOLATE ALMOND COOKIES

You won't believe these are good for you!!

Ingredients:

1 cup almond flour
1 tsp baking soda
1/2 cup Nutiva ® Coconut Manna
1 1/4 cup almond butter
3/4-1 cup honey
2 tsp vanilla
1 egg
3/4 cup unsweetened, vanilla almond milk
1/2 cup unsweetened cocoa powder
12 oz. bag dark chocolate chips

Directions:

1. Preheat oven to 375°F.
2. Combine flour and baking soda in a small bowl and set aside.
3. Cream coconut manna, almond butter and honey in a large bowl until light and fluffy.
4. Add vanilla, egg, almond milk, and cocoa powder and mix until well combined.
5. Stir in chocolate chips.
6. Spoon 2 inch heaps of dough onto a baking sheet and bake for 9-12 minutes.

Serves 10-15

Happiness is the realization of God in the heart. Happiness is the result of praise and thanksgiving, of faith, of acceptance; a quiet tranquil realization of the love of God." Anonymous

LEMON PEACH MERINGUE PIE

A step above the traditional lemon meringue. We think you'll never go back.

Ingredients:

1 Perfect Pie Crust, Pg. 90
6-8 ripe peaches
1/2 cup peach juice and puree (freshly squeezed works best)
1 cup lemon juice
2 tsp finely grated lemon rind
1/2 cup maple syrup
1/2 cup unsweetened, vanilla almond milk
4 tbs arrowroot powder
5 egg yolks

Ingredients for meringue:
5 egg whites
2 tbs maple syrup
1/2 tsp cinnamon

Directions:

1. Preheat oven to 325°F.
2. In a medium sized pan, combine peach puree/juice, lemon juice, lemon rind, and maple syrup and heat on low.
3. Combine almond milk and arrowroot powder in a small bowl and add slowly to peach mixture.
4. Simmer until thickened.
5. Slice half of the peaches in to thin slice and place neatly in pie crust that has been made in a deep dish pie pan.
6. Pour liquid peach mixture over sliced peaches and top with remaining sliced peaches.
7. Add all meringue ingredients to a bowl and beat until stiff. Spoon onto pie top.
8. Bake for 12-15 minutes or until meringue is slightly browned.

Serves 8

"But you, O Lord, are a God merciful and gracious, slow to anger and abounding in steadfast love and faithfulness." Psalm 86:15

APPLE CAKE
A favorite among my kids!

Ingredients:

2 cups almond flour
1/2 tsp baking soda
1/4 cup arrowroot powder
1/4 cup coconut oil
1/2 cup honey
1 Granny Smith apple (or tart apple of your choice) peeled, cored, and diced
1 tbs pure vanilla extract

To prepare cake pans:
1 tbs coconut oil
2 tbs almond flour

Ingredients for Cinnamon Icing:

1/2 cup lite coconut milk
2/3 cup arrowroot powder
4 tbs Nutiva ® Coconut Manna
3 tbs honey
2 tbs maple syrup
2 tsp cinnamon
1 tsp pure vanilla extract

Directions:

1. Preheat oven to 350 °F.
2. Using 1 tbs coconut oil, grease (2) 7-inch pans and "flour" with almond flour. Set aside.
3. Combine all dry ingredients in a medium-sized bowl.
4. In a small bowl, combine wet ingredients. Pour wet ingredients in with dry and stir until just combined.
5. Add apples and stir gently to incorporate apples throughout batter.
6. Pour batter equally into both pans and heat for 20 minutes, or until a toothpick can be inserted into the center of the cakes and removed easily.
7. Allow cake to cool completely before icing.
8. For icing, whisk coconut milk and arrowroot powder in a small bowl until smooth. Add remaining icing ingredients.
9. Frost cake and garnish with leftover apple peels.
10. Refrigerate leftovers...if there are any!

Serves 6-8

"For I know the plans I have for you," declares the LORD, "plans to prosper you and not to harm you, plans to give you hope and a future." Jeremiah 29:11

CHOCOLATE CUPCAKES
Make every day a party with these tasty treats!

Ingredients:

2 1/2 cups almond meal
2 1/2 tsp baking powder
2/3 cup coconut oil
1 1/2 cups honey
1 1/2 tsp vanilla
2 eggs
1 cup almond milk, unsweetened vanilla
1/2 cup melted dark chocolate
1/2 cup unsweetened cocoa powder

Ingredients for chocolate icing:

1 cup dark chocolate
1/2 cup coconut oil
2 tbs honey
1/2 cup arrowroot powder

Directions:

1. Preheat oven to 350°F.
2. Combine flour and baking powder in a large bowl.
3. In a medium bowl, combine eggs, oil, honey, and vanilla.
4. Pour wet ingredients into large bowl and mix.
5. Add melted chocolate and cocoa powder and mix completely.
6. Pour batter into lined cupcake tins and bake for 20 minutes.
7. Allow to cool completely and frost with your favorite icing.

Directions, for chocolate icing:

1. Combine all ingredients in a small pan and heat on low until all are melted, stirring constantly to make sure chocolate does not burn.
2. Pour icing into a food processor and allow to cool for 30 minutes.
3. Whip until light and fluffy.
4. Frost cupcakes.

"God is love. He didn't need us. But He wanted us. And that is the most amazing thing."
Anonymous

BUTTER "GREEN" ICING

Stays great in the refrigerator for up to 3 weeks!

Ingredients:

1 ripe avocado
1 tbs maple syrup
1 1/2 tsb vanilla
3 tbs honey
1 1/2 tbs arrowroot powder
1/2 cup xylitol
1/4 tsp cinnamon

Directions:

1. Combine all ingredients in a food processor.
2. Mix until desired thickness.
3. This icing will be green, but has an incredible flavor very close to a traditional buttercream icing
4. Store in an airtight container in your refrigerator for up to 3 weeks. Despite the avocado, the icing will not brown over time.

"God loves each of us as if there were only one of us." St. Augustine

COCONUT CREAM FROSTING

Frost on your favorite cake!

Ingredients:

1 cup can coconut milk
1 cup xylitol
5 tbs arrowroot powder
1 tbs water
1 1/4 cup coconut oil
1-2 tbs maple syrup

Directions:

1. Heat milk, xylitol, and maple syrup in a small pan for 10-12 minutes.
2. Dissolve arrowroot powder in water and pour into pan.
3. Bring contents in pan to a boil until mixture becomes shiny; making sure to stir constantly.
4. Remove pan from heat and allow to cool for 2-5 minutes.
5. Using a whisk or hand mixer, add coconut oil.
6. Scoop mixture into a bowl and refrigerate until icing is cool and turns white.
7. Remove icing from refrigerator and fluff with a hand mixer until desired texture is achieved.
8. Store unused icing in refrigerator.

"The Lord your God is in your midst, a mighty one who will save; He will rejoice over you with gladness." Zephaniah 3:17

CHOCOLATE PROTEIN COOKIES

Try to stop eating these after just one...we dare you!

Ingredients:

1 cup almond butter
4 oz 100% cacao baker's chocolate, unsweetened
2/3 cup maple syrup
1 tsp vanilla
3 eggs
2 cups almond flour

Directions:

1. Preheat oven to 350°F.
2. Melt chocolate in a small pan over low heat, stirring continually to keep chocolate from burning.
3. In a large bowl mix almond butter and melted chocolate until smooth. Add maple syrup, eggs and vanilla. Stir until smooth.
4. Add almond flour and mix until well combined.
5. Refrigerate for at least one hour.
6. Roll dough into 1-inch balls and bake for 8 minutes on a cookie sheet. Do not over bake. Cool completely on wire racks.

Ingredients for icing:

4 oz 100% cacao baker's chocolate, unsweetened
6-8 tbs maple syrup
1/2 cup almond milk unsweetened vanilla

Directions for icing:

1. Melt all ingredients together over low heat.
2. Remove from heat and allow to cool in a separate bowl.
3. Ice cookies liberally.
4. Store remaining icing in refrigerator. To use after chilled, heat slightly and ice.

"Being confident of this, that he who began a good work in you will carry it on to completion until the day of Christ Jesus." Philippians 1:6

ALMOND AND COCONUT COOKIES
A healthy alternative to an all-time favorite!

Ingredients:

1/2 cup almond butter
2 eggs
1/2 cup unsweetened dried coconut flakes, ground finely
1 tsp baking soda
1 tbs maple syrup
1 tbs honey
1/2 cup dark chocolate chips
1/2 cup dried fruit, optional

Directions:

1. Preheat oven to 320°F.
2. Mix almond butter, eggs, maple syrup, and honey together in a large bowl.
3. In a small bowl, mix coconut flakes and baking soda and pour into large bowl.
4. Stir in chocolate chips and dried fruit.
5. Spoon 1-inch mounds of cookie dough onto a cookie sheet and bake for 10-12 minutes.

Serves 8-10

"Spread love everywhere you go: first of all in your own house. Give love to your children, to your wife or husband, to a next door neighbor... Let no one ever come to you without leaving better or happier. Be the living expression of God's kindness; kindness in your face, kindness in your eyes, kindness in your smile, kindness in your warm greeting." Mother Teresa

BROWNIE POINTS
Score high with these delicious and seriously healthy treats!

Ingredients:

6 tbs coconut oil
1/2 cup maple syrup
1/2 cup unsweetened cocoa powder
1/2 cup pecan meal
1/4 cup arrowroot powder
1 tsp vanilla

Directions:

1. Preheat oven to 350°F.
2. Mix all ingredients together in a medium bowl.
3. Pour batter into a greased 8x8 pan.
4. Bake for 20 minutes or until an inserted toothpick comes out clean.

Serves 10-12

"No one is useless to God. No one, at any point in his or her life, is useless to God -not a little child, not the unattractive, not the clumsy, not the tired, not the discouraged." Max Lucado

ALOHA CAKE

Some say these are better than a day in the Islands!

Ingredients:

1/2 cup pecans
5 ripe peaches
3/4 cup chopped dried pineapple
3/4 cup chopped fresh pineapple
1 tsp apple pie spice
1 tsp cinnamon
2/3 cup pitted dates
1 1/2 cups blueberries
3-4 tbs maple syrup
3-4 tbs Nutiva ® Coconut Manna

Ingredients for crust:

2 1/2 cups almond flour
2/3 cup Nutiva ® Coconut Mana
1 tsp cinnamon

Ingredients , for topping;

1 cup almond flour
1/2 tsp cinnamon
3 tbs Nutiva Coconut Manna
3 tbs maple syrup

Directions:

1. In a small bowl, add pecans and cover with water. Allow pecans to soak for 8-12 hours.
2. After pecans are done soaking, preheat oven to 350°F.
3. In a large bowl, mix crust ingredients together and spread on the bottom of a 9 x 13 greased pan.
4. Peel peaches and reserve the skin. Remove peach pits and cut peaches into thin pieces.
5. Drain pecans.
6. In a food processor, blend peach skins, pecans, fresh and dried pineapple, dates, manna, maple syrup, cinnamon, and apple pie spice.
7. Layer peach slices on crust and spread half of the pecan mixture.
8. Repeat with peaches and pecan mixture.
9. Mix topping ingredients in a bowl and crumble on top of cake.
10. Bake for 30 minutes.
11. Serve hot or cold.

Serves 15-20

"Joy is the most infallible sign of the presence of God." Leon Bloy

BANANA ICE DREAM

You would never know this wasn't ice cream!

Ingredients:

1 cup almond milk, unsweetened vanilla
3 ripe bananas
1 tsp vanilla
1/4 tsp cinnamon
5 tbs maple syrup

Directions:

1. In a blender mix all ingredients until smooth.
2. Put in an ice cream maker and follow ice cream maker directions.
3. If you do not have an ice cream maker, pour liquid ice cream into a freezer-safe container.
4. Place container in freezer, removing every 15 minutes to stir ice cream and break up ice crystals.
5. Continue this process until ice cream is frozen and creamy.
6. Top with unsweetened coconut or cinnamon.

"I came that you may have and enjoy life and have it in abundance, until it overflows." Jesus

VERY BERRY FRUIT SORBET

Sweet, tangy, irresistibly good!

Ingredients:

1 can frozen 100% pineapple orange juice
1 cup frozen berries of your choice
2 cups fresh or frozen strawberries

Directions:

1. In a blender mix all ingredients until smooth.
2. Freeze in a freezer-safe container for 4-6 hours.
3. Garnish with your favorite fruit.

"If you took the love of all the best mothers and fathers who ever lived (think about that for a moment)--all the goodness, kindness, patience, fidelity, wisdom, tenderness, strength and love--and united all those virtues in one person, that person would only be a faint shadow of the love and mercy in the heart of God for you and me." Brennan Manning

COCONUT CUPCAKES

Top with your favorite icing.

Ingredients:

3 eggs
1/2 cup coconut oil
1/2 cup maple syrup
1/2 cup coconut flour
1/2 tsp baking soda
1 tsp vanilla
1/2 cup unsweetened cocoa powder (Optional, add if making chocolate cupcakes)

Directions:

1. Preheat oven to 350°F.
2. Mix wet ingredients in a large bowl.
3. In a small bowl stir together dry ingredients and pour into large bowl.
4. Mix wet and dry ingredients together until well-blended.
5. Pour batter into paper-lined cupcake tins.
6. Bake for 20-25 minutes, or until lightly browned on top.

"Be assured, if you walk with Him and look to Him, and expect help from Him, He will never fail you." George Mueller

COCONUT BREAD PUDDING
An old family favorite!

Ingredients:

3 eggs
1/2 cup unsweetened coconut milk
1/2 cup chopped walnuts, toasted
1/4 cup raisins
1/2 medium apple, chopped
1 tsp cinnamon
1 tsp vanilla
1/2 tsp nutmeg
1 batch of coconut cupcakes

Directions:

1. Preheat oven to 350°F.
2. Grease an 8x8 baking dish.
3. In a small bowl, mix wet ingredients together.
4. Add spices and vanilla.
5. Cut cupcakes into small pieces and place in the bottom of the baking dish.
6. Evenly spread toasted walnuts, raisins, and apples over cupcake pieces.
7. Pour liquid mixture over cupcake pieces in dish.
8. Bake for 35-40 minutes.
9. Allow bread pudding to cool for at least 30 minutes before serving.

Serves 8-10

"The secret of the mystery is: God is always greater. No matter how great we think Him to be, His love is always greater." Brennan Manning

NUTTY BARS

Make ahead and freeze for a fast, energy-filled treat!

Ingredients:

1/4 cup sunflower seeds
1/2 cup pecans
1/2 cup walnuts
1 cup almond flour
2 eggs
2 tbs maple syrup
1/2 tsp cinnamon
1/4 tsp ground ginger
4 oz. dried fruit

Directions:

1. Preheat oven to 350°F.
2. Grease a 9x13 cookie sheet.
3. In a food processor, grind nuts and seeds.
4. Add flour, eggs, syrup, spices, and dried fruit.
5. Spread mixture evenly on cookie sheet and bake for 20 minutes or until edges are slightly browned.
6. Allow to cool for 20 minutes and cut into bars.
7. Store in an airtight container.

Serves 8-10

"In all these things we are more than conquerors through him who loved us." Romans 8:38

ENERGY BALLS

Instant energy!

Ingredients:

1/2 cup almond meal
1/2 cup walnuts, ground
1/2 cup pecan, ground
5-6 prunes
3 tbs coconut oil
1/2 cup raisins
1/2 cup unsweetened cocoa powder
1-2 tbs ground coffee
1/2 cup shredded coconut

Directions:

1. Combine all ingredients together (except the oil) in a food processor.
2. Puree until all ingredients are combined and smooth.
3. Add coconut oil and continue to mix until well combined.
4. Roll into small, bite-sized balls and place on wax paper.
5. Refrigerate for at least one hour.
6. Serve as is, or top with Butter"green" Icing.

Serves 6-8

"God treated me with kindness." Ephesians 3:7a